MY DAD, MY HERO

by

MICHAEL BENTINCK

CONTENTS

© Michael Bentinck 1994

Typeset in 11pt ITC Garamond
and printed on environmentally-friendly paper
by Print-Out, Histon, Cambridge, UK

Cover illustrations © Ronald Searle 1986
From TO THE KWAI AND BACK
(Collins & The Imperial War Museum, London 1986)
By permission of the Tessa Sayle Agency

ACKNOWLEDGEMENTS

My thanks go to Mr Len Baynes, author of 'Kept The Other Side of Tenko', and a fellow Cambridgeshire for his permission for me to mention his bravery at Camp Ban Pong while a prisoner-of-war on the Death Railway.

To my daughter-in-law, Beverley, for her help with spelling and photocopying.

To my mother for passing on to me my father's notes, photos and documents etc, after he passed away, for without them this book would not have been written.

Last of all, to my dear wife Hilary, for all her patience and her encouragement while writing this book and for her idea for the cover.

DEDICATION

The story you are about to read is a true story. It is written from notes kept by my late father and from the things he told me of his experiences in life, especially from the year 1942 until 1946.

It is to honour his memory of the time he spent on this earth that this book is written, and to the memory of all those brave lads in the Cambridgeshire Regiment who served with him, and to those who gave the ultimate sacrifice for their King and Country.

The Cambridgeshires were the last regiment to cease fighting in the fall of Singapore, suffering many fatalities and many wounded. They were known as the Fen Tigers by the other regiments, and my late father was proud to be one of them.

INTRODUCTION

Jim was born in Newnham, Cambridge, at No. 1, South Green Road, on 23rd April 1921, St. George's Day.

He was christened Bernard James Frederick Bentinck, but he was known as Jim. The house overlooked Grantchester Meadows and a University Sports Ground. His father worked as a painter and decorator for one of the colleges and his mother helped at college when she could. Jim was the eldest of two children – he had a younger sister called Margorie. His father's parents lived with them as well, so Jim had plenty of people to care for him and love him. He attended the local village school, but, like most lads, school was not his first love – he would prefer to be playing and getting into mischief with his friends.

Chapter One

CHILDHOOD DAYS

Jim was a well-liked lad. He was always helping people down his street and would often be seen fetching shopping from the village for them. He would chop firewood for them and do gardening for the old ladies who lived on their own, many of them having lost their husbands in the Great War. Jim liked to hear stories about the War and he loved it if his father would tell him about some of the things that happened to him in the War. His father had been in the cavalry, and Jim loved it when his father would let him clean his sabre and boots and stirrups – he would imagine he was getting ready for battle, like the Charge of the Light Brigade. His father would say to him "let's just hope and pray that you never have to go to war, son. It's such a waste of lives." These words would ring in Jim's ears in the years to come.

Jim and his friends would play cowboys and indians and soldiers, and all the games children play, down in Grantchester Meadows. They would swim in the river, have picnics, go fishing, and ice skating in the winter – such a lovely place to grow up. When they played cowboys and indians they would climb the trees and wait 'til the cows or horses that were grazing in the meadows came below them; then they would drop out of the trees on to the animals' backs, and see who could hold on the longest. Jim would think how it must have been for his father having to hold on with one hand while charging with his sabre in the other, 'but then he did have a saddle, stirrups and reins to help him' Jim would think to himself, as he held on for dear life, both arms held tight around the horse's neck. When he got home his mother would say "just look at the state of you, my boy. I hope you've not been up to any mischief." To which Jim would reply "no mum, not me!"

His mother knew only too well what he was like. She knew his favourite game on a Monday morning on his way to school was to open the gate to the meadow and leave it open, so that all the cows got out. He would laugh to himself later that morning. His school teacher would say "do any of you children know how these cows have got into the playground?" "No, miss," he would reply, but he was always one of the first to offer to herd them up and take them back to the meadows.

Jim knew good times and bad times in his childhood days at Newnham. Times were hard – many people were out of work, and he would think how lucky he was. He had many friends, and he had plenty of people to do odd jobs for and earn a penny or two to buy his sweets. Then on one very cold winter's day, he was with some of his friends skating on the river, when one of his friends went through the ice. Jim and his other friends were shocked – it had all happened so quickly. One minute his friend was there and then he was gone. While one friend ran for help, Jim and the others held on to one another and got as close to the hole as they could, but there was no sign of their friend. They knew he had been dragged along under the ice by the strong current.

It was about a week later when the thaw set in that the boy's body was found under the bridge near the Anchor public house. This was the first taste of death for young Jim and to lose a best friend like this was so very hard for him to come to terms with. It had shocked the whole community. Jim saw for himself how all the local community rallied round to help his lost friend's family through those dark days for them. This was something Jim would remember and comfort him in years to come.

Jim was a choir boy at St. Mark's, the Newnham church, and also attended Sunday school there. These things he learned from his young days at church were also to help him through in the years to come.

One day when Jim was on his way home from choir practice he was passing a house where two girls he went to school with lived. On seeing Jim they pressed their faces up against the window to pull faces at him. Young Jim did no more – he just bent down, picked up a stone and threw it at the window. He was as shocked as the girls inside when the window broke, and on hearing their screams took to his toes and rushed home.

"How was choir practice" his mum & dad asked; "not too bad," Jim said, "but what's for supper?" His mother said "you go and wash your hands while I get you some supper." Just as Jim was about to eat his supper there was a loud knock at the front door. His dad said "I wonder who that can be", to which mother replied "if you go and open the door you will find out." Young Jim's heart started to thump fast. He thought to himself 'don't let it be the girls from school and their dad', but sure enough it was. "Hello Mr. Bentinck" the man said. "Is your son Jim at home?" Jim's father said "yes, he has just got in from choir practice." "Well," the man replied, "on his way home my girls inform me he threw a stone at them while they were looking out of our front window, which has broken the window and its only just missed my girls who could have been badly hurt, and of course its made a lot of mess, and I want to know what you are going to do about it." "Jim, get yourself out here this minute" his father called to him. Jim came slowly into the hallway, swallowing down what he thought at that moment might be his last mouthful of food. As the girls saw him they shouted "that's him, dad – he threw the stone." "Well Jim," his father said, "what have you to say for yourself?" "They were pulling faces at me dad I did not mean to break the window but just to scare them a bit." "Well you certainly did that son," the girls father replied, "it's lucky for you they were not hurt. Now what are we going to do about all this then?" Jim's father said "I am a painter & decorator sir, and if its all right with you I will come round tomorrow and put in new glass for you and repaint the window frame for you, and I will also see to it young Jim gets his punishment." Jim's eyes looked at his fathers belt which was around his fathers waist and thought to himself 'that's what I'm in for.' The girls and their father said "goodnight Mr. Bentinck, see you in the morning" and left.

Jim was marched into the front room where he received six of the best he was told that he would receive no pocket money until the price of repairing the window had all been accounted for. He was sent straight to bed feeling very sorry for himself. The next day being Saturday, Jim went with his father to put the new glass in and paint the window. Jim liked this as he loved to be with his father. He apologized to the girls and their father for what he had done , and from that day they all be came good friends and Jim became a frequent visitor to their house.

When Jim was fourteen his time had come to leave school and set out into that big wide world. He got himself a job at the Leys Laundry in Cambridge as a van boy. He was fascinated by cars and engines and could not wait until he could drive himself. He was always asking the man he was with delivering the laundry if he could have a go at driving the van, and it was not long before his wish came true. He soon learnt to drive and soon had a laundry van of his own to drive. He spent a lot of his spare time with the mechanics and soon learnt as much as they did about stripping down engines and rebuilding them – this was to prove so very valuable for Jim in the next few years. Jim's hobby at this time was grass track racing which was done on a wooden framed bike with solid hard tyres, round a grass track. Jim became very good at this and it kept him very fit as well. He won many local races. These bikes had no brakes and one day Jim was off into town to meet his mates when he found his everyday bike had a puncture, so not wanting to be late and miss his mates, he took his grass track bike. He was racing along Hills Road behind a bus using the bus as a wind shield when the bus pulled up sharply at the Catholic church. Poor Jim could do no more but use his feet as brakes, all to no avail. He hit the back of the bus so hard it smashed his wooden framed grass track bike into pieces. Jim ended up being knocked out and had wood splinters in his legs and a pair of worn out shoes. Needless to say he did not meet his mates that day. He soon lost interest in grass track racing after that. He was now eighteen years old and he and his friends had joined the TAs (Territorial Army). They met at the old Drill Hall in East Road, Cambridge. It was now 1938 and at eighteen life seemed good for Jim – he enjoyed being a soldier on a part time basis, he liked the church parades, the training and the comradeship, and he had a girl friend called Dulcie who lived in Impington, a nearby village to Cambridge. They would meet most Saturdays at the Dorothy dance hall, with all their friends and they would go to the pictures together in the week. He also had a steady job and was very happy with his lot. It was now 1939 and Nazi Germany had started to invade through Europe. Jim knew that being in the Territorial Army he would soon be called up. Sure enough it was not long in coming. He heard on the radio that all Territorials must report at once to their units. Jim made his way to the Drill Hall in Cambridge as asked and signed up. He was then billeted in a Mrs. Leader's house in Walkworth Street, Cambridge. He thought to himself 'they could have let me stay at my own home' as it was only a mile away from the Drill Hall, but as Jim knew only to well he was now a full time soldier and must follow orders. It was winter time and Jim and his comrades were sent to Waterbeach picking sugar beet etc. Jim and his mates thought if this is being a soldier we might as well have been farmers – but things would soon change for them. At least they would be able to look back on these days as happy ones! News soon came that they were to be sent to Weighton Hall, Brandon and Kimberley Hall, Norfolk.

Chapter Two

TRAINING FOR WAR

Here at Weighton Hall, Brandon Jim and his comrades did their war training. Most of the chaps enjoyed this – it was hard work but the time passed quickly and at least they all felt like soldiers now, and the food was good although not like good old home, but they got weekend passes sometimes and were able to get home to see friends and family, although all Jim's mates had joined up now – but he was still happy to be home to be with his family and to see his sweet heart. But those weekend passes went too quickly and he was soon back training for warfare. It was at this time that Jim joined the transport section , which was an obvious choice with Jim's love for driving and motor engines. He spent much time driving officers to meetings and met many of his commanding officers this way. He also spent time at Feltwell and Meathwould air fields guarding the planes before moving on to Windom for more warfare training. Then on to the east coast at Backton Seapalling Mundsley putting up wire barricades to keep any German invasion out – also putting land mines along the beaches and making sure security was tight. Just as Jim and his mates were getting used to the east coast, they were moved off again this time to Galashiels in Scotland for more war-fare training , they also spent time in Warwickshire, Nuneton and Coventry, most of the training was now done in full kit and meant running up and down hills. The men were fitter now than they had ever been and they felt like taking anyone on. They heard many rumours and speculation of where they might be going and now they just wanted to get going to wherever they were needed. They felt they had played at being soldiers for long enough and now just wanted the action they had been trained for. Sure enough, they did not have to wait long – they were issued with tropical kit so they knew now that at least it was going to be a hot place. The men chatted amongst themselves of where it could be. Many of them, including Jim, had never been abroad before and they were very excited at this. They were all transported to Liverpool. It was now October 1941 and their time for service to their country had come. They boarded the SS Orcades on a very foggy day and set sail for Canada although none of the chaps knew the destination. While at sea Jim and his mates had more training to do and many of the men were very bad with sea sickness. At last they arrived at Halifax, Nova Scotia, where they boarded the West Point, an American ship which had won the Blue Ribbon some time earlier. They had a long voyage which took them to Trinidad and South Africa where they were allowed some shore leave which passed all to quickly. They soon moved onto Bombay and from there they set sail again not knowing where their destination was to be but after a week at sea they were informed their destination was to be Singapore. They were given maps of all the area and were informed that the Japs had already taken many positions. Many of the men thought they were in a hopeless position and felt they were being thrown into an already lost cause. The ship they were on was one of the fastest so they were first to reach Singapore and landed at Kepel Harbour among much bombing from the Japs with no resistance from any British planes. The men were soon ashore and soon billeted in nearby houses that were in bad repair and many now suffered bomb damage – there was no running water or electricity and the men were told to be suspicious of every object and every foreigner.

Chapter Three

AT WAR

Jim & his mates had arrived. They had been told Singapore was a fortress they were told they were so well protected by large naval guns facing out to sea so the Japanese could not get in, but as history now shows the Japanese advance did not come from the sea but came through the jungle and the Japanese were well trained in jungle warfare. Jim and his mates had been told there would be no surrender and every man must fight to the bitter end – not a very nice thought for a young twenty-one-year-old or any age, but Jim and his mates were fit and well and so full of training they were ready for the action. The first few days were quiet. Jim was kept busy driving supplies about, getting ammunition from the Seletar Aerodrome and getting it to the men who were setting up their own ammunition dumps for their own companies. It was very hot and sticky, something Jim and his mates were not used to. They used to say to one another "we thought we had it rough picking that sugar beet at Waterbeach in the winter weather but it would be nice to be there now, at least we didn't have to put up with these bloody mosquitos". They were given anti mosquito creams but none of the lads could stand the smell of it and many of the chaps said it did not stop them anyway. Things soon started to happen now it was in the first week of February. When our guns started up thousands of shells passed over day and night. No one got much sleep and many tempers frayed through lack of sleep. Many Japs were sighted in the jungle and the men all knew now that the Japs were massing their forces in the jungle ready for the taking of Singapore. The only planes bombing the island were Japanese planes now, and the lads would say to one another "wish our RAF boys would come and blow the little nips out of the sky", but no RAF plane came. One evening, so many lights had been seen on the edge of the surrounding jungle that a young officer called for five volunteers to go with him to see what was going on. Jim, being fed up with just waiting and getting no sleep anyway, did the thing soldiers say never to do – he volunteered. He and the four other volunteers and the young officer darkened their faces, fixed their bayonets, and set off into the jungle. Jim knew he and the others were all scared stiff and on hearing a plane overhead Jim made the whistling noise of a bomb falling. The officer and the other four chaps, thinking it to be the real thing, threw themselves straight down onto the floor of the jungle into all the muck and squalor around them. When they realized that nothing had happened they looked up to see young Jim with a big grin on his face. The young officer said to him, "did you make that bomb whistle noise, Bentinck?" Jim still grinning replied "um, yes sir. I'm sorry, I just did not think. I've heard so many of the bloody things, as soon as I heard the plane I thought 'oh here we go – more bombs coming' and I just made the noise without thinking sir". To which the officer replied "well, Bentinck, you are now on a charge and will be confined to camp. Now lets get back." The very next night the officer and the other four men from the reconnaissance party of the night before went out again with one other volunteer to replace Jim who was confined to camp. These six men were found at daylight near the edge of the jungle all dead. Jim knew he was lucky to be alive at that time, for he surely would have been with them if he had not made that stupid bomb noise. This did not help how he felt for them though – they had given their lives for their King and country and he would remember them as long as he lived. He remembered his father's words when he was a boy – "let's hope you never have to go to war, son", and how he wished he was back home with all his loved ones now.

Things were happening so fast now and Jim and his company had orders to leave the Seletar airfield area, and move to Bukit Timah village area. It was now February 10th and the Japanese were in possession of much of the island. Some 25,000 front-line Japanese troops had landed on the island and the Australian troops were in full retreat. Lieutenant General Percival had the Cambridgeshires dig in at Bukit Timah and Jim found himself digging in on Bukit Timah golf course. There were constant air attacks and heavy bomb-

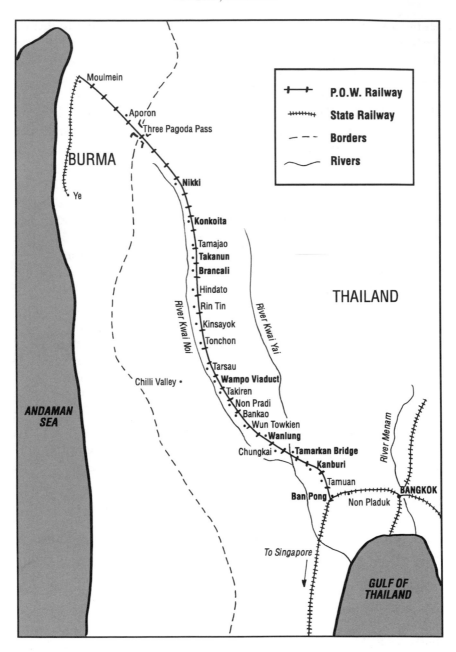

ing and machine gun fire which many men were caught by. It was very upsetting for Jim as many of his mates were the victims of the bombing and machine gun fire. None of the men could see very well as smoke from the bombing and all the burning vehicles had thickened the air so much – many men were physically sick. By now the action was intense and most of the Cambridgeshires' companies were now in the thick of it all at Water Tower Hill, Sime Road, Lornie Road, Adams Park, and the Golf course. By now much of the radio communications between the companies had been lost, and Jim's commanding officer had sent runners to the other companies to ask them all to close in at night. Three runners had already gone and none had returned and so the officer asked for a volunteer. Jim, not being one to want to be in one place too long and thinking to himself that it can't be any more dangerous then staying here, said "I'll go sir." He was given the orders from the officer and set out on his mission. As he came to a clearing at the edge of the jungle he could see the road ahead. There was a burnt out armoured car with two dead bodies laying at the side of it and one half hanging out of the door turret. He knew there could be Jap snipers about and with their camouflage skills he new he would not see them. He also knew he had to cross the road so he thought to himself 'if I can make it to the armoured car I can rest up under it for a breather'. He took in a deep breath and ran as fast as he could towards the armoured car. He had run about 60 yards when he felt as if someone had rabbit punched him in the back of the neck. He fell to the floor as if dead. He lay very still. Now he realized he had been hit by a sniper and he soon realized why the other runners had not come back. He thought to himself that the three other runners could be those laying at the armoured car still some 80 yards further on from were he was. He also realized that he could not feel his left leg. He looked down real slowly, for fear of the Jap sniper seeing him move, and saw that blood was all over him and a large gaping hole was in his groin. He knew that if he did not do something fast he would bleed to death. He decided he must try and drag himself to the armoured car. He thought to himself 'if the sniper does shoot at me again, at least it might be quick for me, and if I just lay here I know I shall bleed to death'. So he slowly pulled himself along toward

15

the armoured car thinking that at any second the Jap sniper would finish him off. He got some twenty yards from the armoured car, and thought to himself 'this Jap is just playing with me unless he can see all the blood and just assumes I'm going to bleed to death anyway'. Jim took one more big breath to make that big effort to cover the last twenty yards and to his amazement he made it. He pulled himself over the dead bodies and got right under the armoured car. He got his field dressing out and plugged the hole in his groin as best he could. He thought from the hole in his left buttock that the bullet must have gone straight through. He lay there thinking to himself 'this is it for me'. He remembered his family and friends back home, especially his fiancé Dulcie, and thought how right they were not to get married before he had set sail – at least she would not have to be a young widow like many of his mates' wives.

He thought also of his childhood – of those happy days playing in the meadows and of his days as a choir boy. He remembered the words of his vicar – 'have faith in God Jim', and as Jim lay there he prayed to his God. As he lay there praying he heard someone running towards him down the road. He looked up to see it was his mate Mick Challis. Jim shouted to him "watch out, Mick, there's a sniper up one of those trees". Jim had no sooner spoken these words when a shot rang out. Mick ran as fast as he could without thinking of the danger. He was zig-zagging as he ran to try to miss the sniper bullets that were now raging down on him. He dived head first under the armoured car, looked at Jim and said "I made it. Thanks for warning me, Jim. You saved my life". Jim said "don't be daft, mate. I'd have done the same for anyone. Anyway," Jim said, "you might be the answer to my prayer". "What's that then, Jim?" replied Mick. "Look at this mess, mate" said Jim. "That bloody sniper's shot me right through the groin. Nearly took me wedding tackle clean off. I think the bullet's gone straight through though, thank God." Mick took his own field dressing and redressed Jim's wounds and managed to stop the bleeding. The Jap sniper was still shooting down at them. Mick said "how we going to get out of this one then, Jim old mate?" Jim said "we have got to get that sniper or he'll keep us pinned down here and it's important that you get through to the other company." The two of them thought for a moment, then Mick said to Jim "I think he must be in one of the tall trees across the other side of the roadway, about 50 yards on from us. I'm going to shoot up at that tall tree, Jim, and see if I can draw his fire down on us. If I can, see if you can get a shot at him." They both crawled on their bellies to the edge of the armoured car. Mick stuck his rifle out and fired at the tree. Sure enough this drew the Jap's fire. He fired back and took the woodwork clean off Mick's rifle but not before Jim had seen where the fire was coming from. Jim let off two quick rounds and they heard a cry as if some one had been hit. They saw a rifle fall from the tree but no body, but they knew by now that Jap snipers tied themselves in the trees and they felt sure Jim must have got him on seeing the rifle drop from the tree. Mick looked at Jim and said "the bloody Jap's taken the woodwork clean off me gun mate." Jim could see this had shocked Mick and said "don't worry old mate. He won't be shooting down at any one else. The birds can have him, mate. Now you must get through to B & C Companies." "But I can't leave you like this, old mate" Mick replied with tears in his eyes, for the two had been mates back home in England. Mick lived in Shelford, just a couple of miles from where Jim lived in Newnham. Jim said "come on, mate, you can worry about me later. You must get going." Mick said "soon as I get through, mate, I'll get you picked up." He left Jim all the rest of his field dressing, and the two men embraced one another and, tears running down their faces they said goodbye to one another, for in their hearts they knew they might never see one another again. Jim said "if you don't see me again, Mick, tell my Dad I gave it my best, and tell my Dulcie to be happy and tell her I love her." "Come on, Jim", Mick replied, "don't you get like that. You're going to tell them yourself, mate – when we get these Japs sorted out." With that, Mick took off zig-zagging down the road. Jim lay watching him until he was out of sight. Jim lay there for what seemed like hours to him for Jim was not one to stay in one place for long at the best of times. He felt so cold as he lay there. He could hear the sounds of the guns and bombs going off. He soon slipped in to unconsciousness. Hours later, some retreating Australians came across the armoured car and, lucky for Jim, found he was still alive.

The Australian soldiers took him with them , and when Jim came to he was in Singapore Hospital. He saw he had a tube going into his arm and a bottle hanging above him from where the tube was coming from. A nurse said to him "hello there – you thought you would wake up then." Jim said "what's all this? Where am I?" The nurse replied "you're alright. You're in hospital and that's a blood transfusion. You have been shot through the groin and the bullets gone straight through and has come out your left buttock – a nice clean wound, though. You will soon be up and about again." Jim asked about his company and was informed that they had suffered many losses but they were still holding out at Adams Park, but the situation was getting very grim now; many areas of the city were burning, there was now no running water, and the Japanese Air Force were able to do as they liked now with no British planes to oppose them, most of the roads were blocked with burnt out vehicles, and the smell of burning smoke, was everywhere. The nurse told Jim "I'm sorry we are so over crowded but we have no where else. Jim could see many of the wounded just laying in the corridors, also many dead bodies just lay heaped up waiting for burial parties to attend to them. He later found out that the hospital had dug two large mass graves to bury the dead in as there were so many of them. It was not long before the Japanese took the hospital. The hospital Medical Officer Lieut. Weston went to the rear of the hospital where the Japanese soldiers had gathered. He carried with him a white flag but the Japanese soldiers took no notice of this and bayoneted Lieut. Weston to death. The Japanese soldiers then entered the hospital and ran amok; they entered the ward Jim was in and the Jap officer ordered that the person in every other bed be killed by bayoneting them. Once again Jim was lucky and happened to be in the safe bed , but he was in a state of shock now at seeing just how cruel the Japanese were. The Japanese soldiers killed many of the doctors and nurses as well taking no notice of their Red cross brassards, they even burst in to an operating theatre where an operation was in progress. They did not wait for a moment – just bayoneted the doctors and nurses and the patient as he lay on the operating table. Jim and those that they had left alive were rounded up, whatever medical condition they were in, their hands tied, then forced in to small outbuildings. The room Jim was forced into was about 12' x 12' and about 70 people were forced into this room – they were crammed in like sardines in a tin. There was no room left to sit down, only to stand, many of the others had under gone amputations, and those that could were holding them up. The heat was unbearable they were given nothing to drink and now and then the Japs would take two or three outside and bayonet them to death. Many of the nurses were taken and were raped before being bayoneted to death. Jim thought it would not be long before his turn of being pulled out by the Japs would come; he spent that night packed tight in the room and things were very quiet – no sign of the Japs but they could hear the fighting going on. Later that day it all went quiet – the sound of mortars bombing stopped for it was February 15th 1942 and General Percival had signed the Surrender at 19.30 hours that evening. The Japanese had taken Singapore. It was on the 16th, the next day, that Jim and his fellow captors were let out, but this time it was by different Japanese soldiers. They seemed much smaller and their commanding officer informed the captors that they had been captured by soldiers of the Japanese Imperial Guards division, who had now moved on. British officers told the Japanese officer of the dreadful atrocities they had suffered at the hand of the Imperial Guard only to be told they must keep quiet and that they were now to be guests of the Great Japanese Emperor. Jim had some how survived the massacre of Alexandra Hospital; he was taken to another hospital under Japanese guard and was left there for a few days to get over his wounds and the shock he had been through over the last few days.

Chapter Four

CAPTIVITY IN CHANGI

Jim was still in a state of shock, and the hospital he had been taken to was so overcrowded he did not have a bed; he lay on an old hospital trolley in the corner of the ward. The stench was so bad it made him feel sick, many of the wounded did not get their dressings changed through lack of new dressings; sheets, towels etc were all used as dressings. Jim's wound was healing OK now and he lay wondering what was going to happen to him now. He wished something could be done about the flies that were everywhere. He had been told that water was scarce and what they did have had to be boiled and that the food was running out as well. As the days passed Jim was able to walk about a little and get some strength back in his legs; by doing this he met up with many of his friends from his 1st. Cambridgeshires 'A' Company and they exchanged stories of how the past days had been for them. Jim was told how the Cambridgeshires had been among the last to surrender and that many of his close mates had been killed. He was told that the part where he was dug in took a direct hit and the chaps who had been with him were all killed; one of the chaps said "so it looks like you did the right thing, Jim old mate, by volunteering to be a runner. At least you're still alive." Jim thought to himself 'yes, but for how long.' He explained to his chums just how wicked the Japanese could be and that they had no respect for any one but themselves. Jim told them how on the way out to Singapore he had bought a gold ring and necklace for his fiancé Dulcie and that the Japanese had taken these from him. This was to be one thing he could never forgive them for. Now that Jim could move about he was soon sent to Singapore's Changi prison. He and many of the others were forced to march to the prison. Some of the men had suffered leg amputations and they were not at all fit enough for such a journey; those that could get along helped those that could not. One chap near to

Jim fell down; he had suffered a broken leg and arm, and broken ribs in the last few days of the fighting. Jim bent to help him up as he bent down he was kicked up the back side and fell over himself. As he looked round he saw a little fat Japanese guard glaring at him saying "you no help him – he get up himself." Jim got up and stood back in line. As his comrade tried to get up the Jap guard kicked him down again by actually kicking at his broken leg. Many of the prisoners moved forward towards the Jap guard but more guards aimed their guns at them and shouted at them to stay in line. The guard then carried on beating the other chap and as he lay on the ground all the Jap guards were laughing at this poor man's suffering. A British officer came forward and shouted at the Jap guard to stop. For his trouble the officer was hit full in the face by a rifle butt by one of the other Jap guards, but at least the chap on the ground was now left alone. The others in the party were ordered by the Japs to pick him up and carry him the rest of the way to Changi prison. The guards had had their fun at the expense of this poor man – he was unconscious and the others feared for his life.

On arrival at Changi the men were so tired that they just collapsed. The men already at Changi came and helped them. They were taken to the sick bay, which was no more then a shambles – the medical staff had no medication for the men, and so all they could offer them was rest, but this was good medicine for Jim and after a couple of days he felt much better. They had been allocated food that had been collected up from their own British food dumps, and thanks to this and the rest, Jim was soon back to health. He soon found his way about camp and quickly found where it was safe to go and where not to. He met up now with many more of his own company, the Cambridgeshires. As they were among the last to surrender the Japanese had held them in closed-in tennis courts for some time before bringing them to Changi prison. The prison had been built to hold about 600 prisoners but the Japanese had cramped some 9,000 men into it. Needless to say, conditions were very bad – food was beginning to run out, and the Japanese had now issued new food rations – twelve ounces of rice a day. Many of the men thought 'that wont be to bad, I like rice pudding' but they were remembering the puddings their mothers and wives had made for them, but they were to receive just plain rough rice with husks – not really fit for human consumption. On getting his first allowance of this Jim received about a half a tea cup full. Illness was now starting to break out all over the place; men were dropping like flies – there were no proper toilets working, just the latrines the men had dug themselves. Most of the men were suffering from dysentery and malaria attacks for which the British medical staff had very little medication and the Japanese would not give them any, so sickness and hunger were now the main problem; morale was low as the Japanese made the men watch while they executed three prisoners who were found outside the camp's perimeter fencing. This was a very sad time indeed.

It was now the end of March and the commanding officer of the 'A' company of the Cambridgeshires died of the wounds he received in the last few days of battle. The men who were fit enough attended his funeral and Jim thought of his first meeting with the officer when he had driven him to meetings back in Cambridge and how he had spoken of his family. Jim's prayers were with his family at this time for they had lost a brave loved one and Jim and his comrades had lost a fine commanding officer. It was now that the Japanese ordered work parties of the prisoners to work at the railway station and at the docks. Jim was allocated to one of the work parties and marched to the docks where he was to see more cruelty dished out by the Japanese and Indian guards, most of whom were Sikhs and Bengalis and had a great dislike of the British, which Jim and his comrades were to find out to their cost. One day while unloading rice from a ship, Jim was pushed by one of the guards and he fell on to one of the other guards, dropping the sack of rice on him. Jim was given a very bad beating by the guards and was left for dead. His comrades were sure the guards had killed him. He did not move, just laying there in the full heat of the sun. At the end of the day's work the guards did allow Jim's comrades to carry him back to the prison where he was handed over to the medical boys who nursed him back to life. Many of the men gave up their food ration so that those who were in the hospital unit could have extra; also men would risk their lives by leaving the camp at night and getting under the wire fences and going to the local shops, houses etc to pinch food or if they had any money they would barter with the local people with it to buy food. Many of the men did this for the sick, not just for themselves – Jim received his share of this food and was so glad of it. He never would forget the bravery of these men.

One of Jim's mates from the Cambridgeshires would risk his life most nights to get food for his fellow Cambridgeshires. On one of his night sorties he came across some local natives who had some chickens. He hid up 'til all was quiet and made his move on one of the chickens. He thought to keep it quiet he would chop its head off, but as he told his story to Jim and his other mates in the Changi hospital unit the medical chaps asked him to leave, as he was causing to much discomfort to the patients by making them laugh too much – for when he chopped the chicken's head off, the chicken had got up and run off and the commotion had woken the natives and he himself had to run for his life and sneak back into camp empty handed, but he just could not make out how the chicken could run about once he had chopped his head off. His mates told him even though he had brought no food back for them, the story had been a tonic for them all – they had not laughed so much for a long time. Although it hurt every bone in Jim's body where the Jap and Indian guards had beaten him, he still felt better for a good laugh, as there was certainly not much for them to laugh about now. Jim was starting to recover from his beating but was suffering from very bad dysentery and malaria. The hospital unit and any likely mosquito nesting areas were allowed to be sprayed with anti-malaria vaccine. Cholera broke out, which frightened the Japs so much they allowed men to be vaccinated against it but still it took many lives. One day as Jim lay suffering, a Japanese officer with two guards came into the hospital unit. The officer asked the doctor in charge which of the men could drive. The doctor soon found out and quickly showed these men to the Japanese officer. The officer looked over the men and came to where Jim lay on an old bamboo bed. In his broken English he said to the doctor "this man be OK?". The Doctor explained to the officer that Jim could be all right if he had the right medicine, to which the Jap officer replied "I get you medicine for this man – you have him ready for me in two days."

The doctor told him that it would take more then two days for this man to be able to drive. The Jap officer looked at the doctor with stern face and replied "two days – or else. I get medication for you now. You will have him ready." Then the Jap officer left. The doctor tried to calm Jim down for Jim was worried what was in store for him. One of the guards returned with the medicines and gave them to the doctor. The doctors and the men were all talking about how the Japs could supply medicine if it was to their benefit. Jim said to the doctors "share the medicine on the chaps who are worse then me," but the doctors said "Jim, we must try and get you up and going. We have two days so take your medicine and lets see if we can improve you." They warned him if he received another beating it would most certainly kill him. Jim did as he was asked and started to walk around the ward as best he could. The medicines started to help his dysentery and this made him feel much better and food started to nourish him a bit although he had lost four stone since arriving in Singapore. He was still so very weak but after two days the Jap officer was back for him. The officer only stood about 4' 10" and Jim was 6'. The Jap officer had a long samurai sword and Jim thought to himself how the sword was as big as he was. The officer said to Jim "you come with me now. You do as I say, you be OK." Jim walked off with the officer as best he could, still feeling so ill and only wearing all that he had to his name – a pair of old shorts and vest. He was taken to an old vehicle similar looking to a jeep. The Jap said to him "you drive this?". Jim said "yes, I can drive this". The Jap officer got in the passenger seat and two Jap Guards sat behind him.

Chapter Five

RIVER VALLEY CAMP

Jim got in the drivers seat and started up the engine thinking to himself 'this sounds about had it'. The Jap officer said to Jim "speedo benji" so Jim drove off. He was soon to find out what 'speedo benji' meant – it meant you go flat out! As soon as they hit any open road the Jap officer would start shouting out at the top of his voice "speedo benji". Jim would put his foot to the floor and just let the thing go as fast as it could.

After the first few weeks of driving the Jap officer about, Jim found out what the officer's job was – he was an executioner. He would execute Chinese, Malayans, Indians, and some British prisoners if they were found trying to escape or looting. Their hands would be tied behind their backs, they would be knelt down, then that big samurai sword would chop off their heads, which Jim would have to place on poles and leave on show for locals to see as a warning to them not to loot etc. Jim had to dispose of the bodies; he had to dig a large mass grave with some of the other prisoners on the edge of River Valley camp just outside the perimeter fence into which the bodies were put and then covered with lime. One day while they were out, they passed a young Indian just standing on the edge of the road. The executioner shouted at Jim to stop. He and the two guards got out of the vehicle, grabbed the Indian, bent him over and chopped his head off. Jim sat in the drivers seat mesmerised. It had happened so quick and without any reason. Jim felt sure the Japs had just grabbed him and done it just for their own sick fun. The Japs just got back in and told Jim to put the body in the back and place the head on a bamboo pole which Jim carried in the truck with them. Jim did this feeling sick to his stomach as he did most times. He was still very weak himself as all he received was a couple of cups of rice a day, and he was suffering from skin ulcers through lack of vitamins. One day the Jap officer stopped at a local

Malayan-run shop and strutted inside; Jim followed him in and seeing all the food his mouth watered. The Jap officer picked up a
fresh fruit pie and a tin of fruit to which the shop keeper just did
not say anything. Jim seeing this and feeling so weak and hungry
picked up a fruit pie and put it in his shirt; the shop keeper saw this
and went to the Jap executioner ranting on to him what Jim had
done. Jim thought 'this is it – I'm done for now', but to Jim's amazement the Jap just pushed the shop keeper away and walked out of
the shop. Jim walked out behind him. As they got down the front
porch of the shop, the Jap turned round and hit Jim full round the
face. Jim fell straight down and curled him self into a ball fearing
the beating to follow, but it never came. The Jap officer spoke in
Japanese to the two guards still sitting in the back of the truck they
got out and picked Jim up. Jim was sure they were to hold him
while the officer executed him, but they picked him up and sat him
in the driver's seat and the officer said "drive on, Jim". Jim thought
to himself 'perhaps none of them can drive so they are just letting
me live 'til we get back to camp'. On arrival back at camp he stopped
as usual to let the Japs out and was amazed to just be allowed to go.
He walked slowly back to the atap hut where he told his mates of
what he had done, and they shared the fruit pie together. The next
morning Jim, as usual, got the truck and picked up the Japanese
officer and guards and nothing was said. Sometimes from then on,
the Jap officer would place a can of fruit under Jim's seat and tell
him "if you can get it into camp you can have it". Jim could not
make out how this Jap could just kill people with out any thought
yet he could show kindness to Jim in this way.

Jim sat one evening talking to his mates exchanging what they
had been doing that day, when a new face appeared in the hut. It
was a chap Jim had been in the hospital unit at Changi with. He
joined Jim and his mates chatting and they spoke about their march
they had made to Changi and how the guards had beaten their comrade. Jim was saddened to hear from the new man that this chap
had died from the effects of the beating some few days after arriving
at Changi. Jim realized just how lucky he had been to survive his
beating and wondered to himself if he would still be alive today if it
was not for the Jap executioner needing him to drive him about.

For now he was getting the odd tin of fruit to mix with his rice. Jim spent the next five months driving the Jap executioner about and the sights he had to endure would stay in his mind for the rest of his life.

Towards the end of his time with the executioner, Jim's health was suffering – he had constant attacks of dysentery and malaria and some days he could hardly manage to drive the truck as he was so weak, but at least he was able to sit down while driving – not like his other mates back at camp, who were suffering beatings by the Jap guards most days while working in work parties on the roads, at the docks etc. At least the Jap executioner was kind to him. He only hit Jim the once when Jim had taken the fruit pie. Jim was lucky enough to be given his water ration each day by one of the Jap guards who travelled with Jim and the executioner. Jim was glad of this as the water back at River Valley camp that the men had to drink was not good. A river ran at the edge of the camp but the water was so dirty and stagnant, needless to say all water was boiled in the camp before consumption, although the food was to be some of the best Jim was to receive in his three and a half years as a guest of the Japanese Emperor. The brave lads who risked their lives sneaking out of camp at night to get food would bring it back for the cooks who would prepare a special meal some nights when stocks permitted. The Jap guards turned a blind eye mostly, and the chaps were able to have one good meal with some meat at least once a week. For many of them it was this one meal that kept them alive as many of the men just could not stomach the rice day in, day out – it was of such poor quality many of the men just sicked it back up, so having that one good meal a week was a godsend. Even those too ill to eat much would try their hardest to eat. For those who were so ill that they could not eat, the cooks would make a broth from the chicken stock for them; just to sip what they could was some help to them. So many men owed so much to the brave few who risked their lives to bring extra food into camp to share with their comrades. One of these men was Fred Jones from the village of Cottenham in Cambridgeshire, about 5 miles from where Jim's home was in Newnham. The chaps nicknamed him Jona, and many men owed their lives to his bravery, but as he said, he was just one of

27

many who took the risks to help his mates. One morning when Jim reported to the executioner there was a line of six lorries behind the truck that Jim drove the executioner in. As Jim set off, the lorries followed in line behind him; Jim wondered what was going on. The Jap executioner ordered Jim to drive to a nearby wood yard that Jim had passed many times before; it was run by local Malayans. Jim pulled in, the lorries still behind him, and the Jap executioner got out and found the man in charge of the woodyard. Jim could hear the Malayan ranting back at the Jap executioner but he had no idea what was being said. The Malayan was shouting and waving his arms about. Jim looked on in amazement when the Jap executioner pulled out that Samurai sword and just swung at the Malayan taking his two arms off clean at the elbows. The Jap executioner then signalled to the guards in the six lorries who then just machine-gunned down all the rest of the workers in the timber yard. The guards then loaded the six lorries with all the wood and machinery that was in the yard. While they were doing this Jim had to drive the executioner and the two guards who travelled with him, and the boss of the timber yard who was now missing two arms, to the local village square. The two Jap guards mustered up all the locals they could find and while they watched, the man was beheaded. Jim then had to place his head on a pole and load what was left of the man onto the truck and take it to the burial pit for disposal. Three more local woodyards were dealt the same blow that day, all suffering the same fate. Jim was twenty one years old and the sights he was seeing each day were taking their grip of him; he would wake up in the night shouting and screaming through nightmares of the things he had witnessed during the day. This used to wake the other men, who realized he was getting worse. They spoke to the officer in charge of their unit who then spoke to Jim about it and decided Jim had had enough of it, and he would speak to the Japanese executioner to explain that Jim was now too ill to drive him any more. This is what he did and so six months of being with the executioner were now over for Jim. When Jim placed the dead bodies in to the mass grave, he always said a prayer for them and a bible reading from an old army bible that one of the chaps had managed to keep. The reading was from Revelations chapter 21 verse 1 to 9, then he would sing his favourite hymn, 'Abide With Me'. His mates used to say to him "for people you don't know, Jim, you give them a good send off", to which Jim would reply "there but for the grace of God go I".

Jim was allowed to spend the next few days in camp trying to get over his attack of malaria and dysentery. It was during this time that the Japanese allowed Jim and his mates to send a post card home; many of the men said "it's not worth the bother, the nips won't send them off any way", but Jim sent his hoping in his heart of hearts it would reach his family back home in Newnham. He was allowed to just put 'I am well and being well cared for and hope you are all well' and that was it. Many of the men complained how unfair it was that they could not write what they wanted to, but Jim knew how cruel the Japanese were and even though it was not what he wanted to say he new at least his family would know he was still alive. Soon after this time the Japanese announced they were to build a railway to transport their troops to Burma. The railway was to run from Thailand through dense jungle through to Burma, and the Japanese told the British officers that the prisoners were to build it under the instructions of their own Japanese engineers. When Jim heard of this he soon realized why all the timber yards had been taken over.

The next few days saw much confusion as men were rounded up to leave River Valley. Many of the men Jim had got to know while in River Valley camp were mustered up and sent off to Japan. Jim wondered if he would be sent, but then early one morning Jim and his mates were rounded up and split up into parties of twenty five men. They were then loaded on to trucks and taken to a railway station about two hours drive away. Jim was so pleased that they were not force marched as he was still suffering from malaria and dysentery and now a touch of beri-beri, and he knew he would not make it anywhere if he had to walk. His mates helped him from the truck and into the steel railway trucks which felt like ovens with the hot sun beating down on them.

Chapter Six

OFF TO THAILAND

The trucks were about twelve or fourteen foot long by about six feet wide. Thirty five men were pushed into these trucks; there was not room to lie down and stretch out, not even room to sit down properly; the floors of the trucks were covered in excreta with flies everywhere. The guards informed the men the journey would take about six or seven days. As they set off, Jim thought to himself 'I'm going to be lucky if I make it'. The door of the truck was a sliding door, and at least with this open some breeze came into the truck; if the men standing near the sides of the trucks caught their bodies on the metal sides, the heat from the metal was so hot they suffered bad skin burns, so it was taken in turns to stand near the sides. Those men who were too ill to stand for long were allowed to lay down for a short time while the rest of the men huddled even closer together to make more room. When nature called men were held by their mates while their backsides hung out of the door way; those like Jim with dysentery soon found who their mates were, but to urinate was not so bad although some times it did blow back at them. With no toilet paper or any washing facilities the men smelt badly; they were allowed to stop twice a day for meals which was once again rice with some type of stew but no one could find meat in it, just a runny gravy, washed down with a small drop of water, then after about half an hour they would be off again. As night fell it would get very cold, and after the heat of the day men would shiver with cold – it was the only time men were glad to be huddled to-gether to keep warm. There was no way anyone could sleep so men took it in turns to tell one another about their lives back home and of their families.

Jim made many more friends through these days and was proud to tell them the story of his life so far, and it made him feel good to talk about his loved ones back home; how he wished he was with them now. After about four nights and five days of the journey, they arrived at Ban Pong, the end of their train journey. They were allowed out of the trucks and the men felt good just to stretch their legs and to catch up with friends from other trucks. They were all handed over to a fresh lot of guards. All counted by the new Jap guards, the men were marched off to their new camp. The locals watched the men as they marched through Ban Pong village. There were many shops, and Jim and his mates joked to one another how it would be nice of the locals to bring them out something nice to eat, but no such luck.

When they reached the camp it was more like a swamp – black, slimy mud everywhere, which stank so much it made even those who were not sick start to feel sick. There was raw sewage floating about and swarms of large bluebottle flies everywhere. The huts were all in such a bad state of repair the men wondered if it was worth trying to fix them up. The men had to wait while a fellow p.o.w. who had passed away that morning was taken out from one of the huts. The new men all said to one another "if we don't get this place cleaned up, that's how we shall all go out of this camp". It was just uninhabitable. The men set to and cleaned up the huts as best they could using leaves from the trees as brushes. After making up beds from more dry leaves they laid down for the night. Jim thought how good it was to be able to lay down and stretch out again, and he soon drifted off to sleep, not because of the pleasant surroundings he found him self in but just through sheer exhaustion.

When he awoke early next morning he helped the meal orderlies get breakfast. Some of the men had some Red Cross issue they had brought with them from Changi which they reluctantly handed over to make up the poor rations the men had, and the men received a good breakfast far better than they had for some time. After breakfast, work parties carried on trying to clean up the camp; the men found a large well to get water from but it was not like the wells we know – it had a long bamboo pole that went down into the well with buckets attached to it which often fell off when trying to get water up. Len Baynes of the Cambridgeshires (known to his mates as Snowy because of his white hair and his white beard, although he was only twenty three years old) lowered himself down the well and retrieved the buckets, for which his mates were thankful as they had very few buckets to carry water from the well to the huts, and at this time every bucket was precious as there were not many buckets in the camp. Many of the men were able to buy fruit from Thai traders who came to the camp fence even though the Jap guards beat them off. Jim was so pleased to get some bananas he ate three of them straight away and was pleased to keep them down. The men were allowed to go in parties to the nearby river to swim, all naked of course, which amused the local Thai girls who watched them, but the men did not mind this one bit. They joked with one another how if they did not feel so week they would be only to pleased to chase the girls and give them something to remember them by, but it was just so good to feel clean again; many of the chaps had worn their clothes out by now and had to make do with any old rags they could lay their hands on to make something like a baby's nappy to wear which they called Jap happys; these the men washed out while at the river then while they swam they laid them out to dry in the heat of the day.

After three days at Ban Pong the men were rounded up and loaded into lorries which were not as bad as the railway trucks with their steel sides. The men were taken to a camp on the outskirts of Kanchanburi. Jim was pleased to be leaving Ban Pong; he thought how right the name pong was for it – he had never smelt anything like it and was glad to be away from the sight of raw sewage floating about. On arrival they were informed that they would only be stopping for one night and they were given their usual rice ration to which Jim added one of his bananas. After the meal they found themselves somewhere to lay for the night. The next morning they were up early to find it raining very hard and they were rounded up and marched off through the town. They marched for some miles before coming to a river, where they were split into small groups and boarded onto barges which took them across the river. On reaching the other side they could see that they were leaving any sign of civilization behind them – all they could see ahead of them was jungle. It was still raining hard as they were marched off into the jungle; the Jap guards cut their way through the thick jungle growth

Jim's mum and dad.

Jim with his work van outside 1 South Green Road, Newnham before the war.

Dad in uniform with mum just before he sailed for the far east

Dad in uniform in back yard at South Green Road.

Jim and Dulcie on their wedding day at Impington Church in 1946.

Jim and Dulcie on their honeymoon.

Jim and Dulcie on a day out soon after coming home.

The Chunsaki Pass cut through a rock hillside by hand. *(Vic Brown Collection)*

Viaduct constructed from teak at Wampo. Jim's mate was pushed from it while working on repairs to it. *(Vic Brown Collection)*

Jim in a very rare group photo taken at River Valley Camp 1942. Circled are Jim and the executioner for whom he acted as driver.

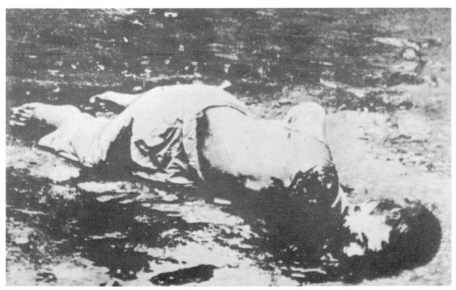

Street scene in Japanese-occupied Singapore, typical of the atrocities Jim witnessed and had to 'clear up'.

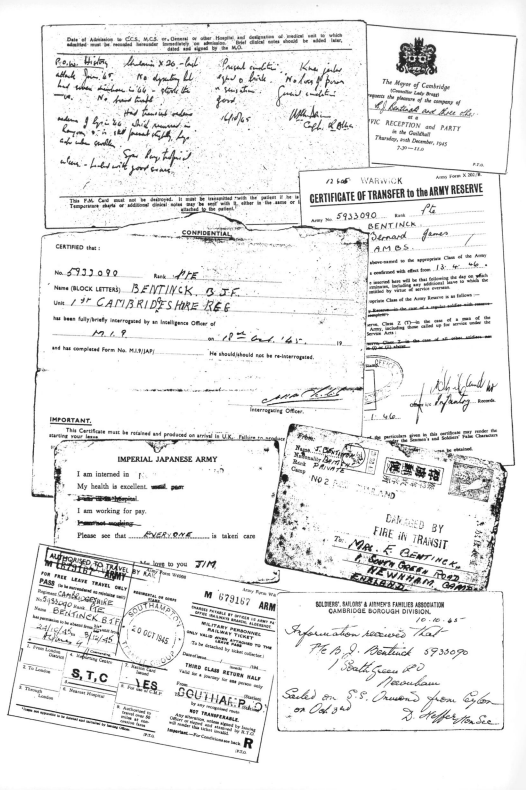

Date of Admission to C.C.S., M.C.S. or General or other Hospital and designation of medical unit to which admitted must be recorded hereunder immediately on admission. Brief clinical notes should be added later, dated and signed by the M.O.

P.O.W. History. Malaria X 20 - last
attack June '45. No dysentery but
had severe diarrhoea in '66 - since the
—ve. No bowel trouble.
orders 9 Aug '46. Shid returned in
Rangoon & is still present slight, Eye
ache when swollen.
Present condition
eyes & ankle
" sensation
Good condition.
14/10/45
Knee jerks
No loss of power
General condition
good.
With. Aim.
Capt. R Obhn.

This F.M. Card must be destroyed. It must be transmitted with the patient if he is
Temperature charts or additional clinical notes may be sent with it, either in the same or
attached to the patient.

The Mayor of Cambridge
(Councillor Lady Bragg)
requests the pleasure of the company of
B J Bentinck and three others
at a
CIVIC RECEPTION and PARTY
in the Guildhall
Thursday, 20th December, 1945
7.30—11.0
P.T.O.

12 405   WARWICK   Army Form X 202/B.
CERTIFICATE OF TRANSFER to the ARMY RESERVE
Army No. 5933090   Rank   Pte
BENTINCK
Bernard James
A.M.B.S.
above-named to the appropriate Class of the Army
confirmed with effect from   13. 4. 46
inserted here will be that following the day on which
terminates, including any additional leave to which the
entitled by virtue of service overseas.
propriate Class of the Army Reserve is as follows :—
Reserve—in the case of a regular soldier with reserve
complete.
serve, Class Z (T)—in the case of a man of the
Army, including those called up for service under the
Service Acts.
Class Z—in the case of all other soldiers
(i) or (ii) above.
Officer i/c Infantry Records.
1. 46

CONFIDENTIAL

CERTIFIED that :

No. 5933090   Rank   PTE
Name (BLOCK LETTERS)   BENTINCK, B.J.F.
Unit   1st CAMBRIDGESHIRE REG
has been fully/briefly interrogated by an Intelligence Officer of
M.I.9   on   18th Oct. '45.   19
and has completed Form No. M.I.9/JAP/   He should/should not be re-interrogated.

Interrogating Officer.

IMPORTANT.
This Certificate must be retained and produced on arrival in U.K. Failure to produce
starting your leave.

particulars given in this certificate may render the
the Seamen's and Soldiers' False Characters
be obtained.

IMPERIAL JAPANESE ARMY

I am interned in
My health is excellent. usual. poor.
I am ill in hospital.
I am working for pay.
I am not working
Please see that   EVERYONE   is taken care
My love to you   J/M.

From:
Name J. BENTINCK
Nationality British
Rank PRIVATE
Camp
NO 2   THAILAND

DAMAGED BY
FIRE IN TRANSIT

To: MRS. E. BENTINCK,
1 SOUTH GREEN ROAD
NEWNHAM, CAMB
ENGLAND

AUTHORISED TO TRAVEL
BY RAIL
M 675167   ARMY   Army Form W4098
FOR FREE LEAVE TRAVEL ONLY
PASS (to be surrendered on rejoining unit)
Regiment CAMBRIDGESHIRE
No 5933090 Rank PTE
Name BENTINCK B.J.F.
has permission to be absent from his
24/11/45 to 3/12/45
Time 4
1. From London   4. Reporting Centre
District
2. To London
S.T.C
3. Through   6. Nearest Hospital
London
*Items not applicable to be deleted and initialled by Issuing Officer.

REGIMENTAL OR CORPS
STAMP
SOUTHAMPTON
20 OCT 1945
TRANSIT GROUP

M 679167   ARM
CHARGES PAYABLE BY OFFICER I/C ARMY PA
OFFICE (RAILWAYS BRANCH) ALDERSHOT.
MILITARY PERSONNEL
RAILWAY TICKET
ONLY VALID WHEN ATTACHED TO THE
LEAVE PASS
(To be detached by ticket collector.)
Date of issue
(month)   /194
THIRD CLASS RETURN HALF
Valid for a journey for one person only
From
SOUTHAMP.D
(Station)
To
(Station)
NOT TRANSFERABLE.
Any alteration, unless signed by Issuing
Officer or signed and stamped by R.T.O.
will render the ticket invalid.
Important.—For Conditions see back.
R
P.T.O.

Army Form W
5. STC
7. Ration Card
Issued
8. For use of C.M.P.
9. Authorised to travel over 50
miles at con-
cession fares
(P.T.O.)

SOLDIERS', SAILORS' & AIRMEN'S FAMILIES ASSOCIATION
CAMBRIDGE BOROUGH DIVISION.
10.10.45
Information received that
Pte B.J. Bentinck 5933090
1 South Green Rd
Newnham
Sailed on S.S. Ormond from Ceylon
on Oct 3rd
D. Heffer Hon Sec

Prisoners carrying rice, Saraburi, Thailand

Jim holding a snake on his visit back to Thailand,
probably thinking of how he used to eat them!

Jim and his fellow security guards at the Cambridge Evening News.

When "News" security officer Jim Bentinck won a giant Easter egg in a local pub competition he decided to spread the fun around.

Yesterday he and his wife Dolcy took the £29 egg to the children's ward at Addenbrooke's Hospital, Cambridge, to be shared among the children.

Mr Bentinck won the egg in a competition organised to raise money for MAGPAS at the Black Horse pub at Histon.

He said: "I have got grandchildren but they all had eggs of their own and it would probably have been wasted so I thought it would be nice to give it to the kids at the hospital."

(Photos: courtesy of the Cambridge Evening News)

until they reached a path already cut, which they followed for some miles, many of the men receiving beatings for not keeping up. They soon reached a clearing where they could see atap huts made out of bamboo with thatched roofs – they had reached Chungkai Camp. Once more they sorted out a place to sleep in the huts and prepared a meal of rice and fruit. Again they met men already at the camp and they told them of the cruelty dished out by the guards and that the guards were mostly Koreans in the camp with Japanese guarding all the work parties.

Chapter Seven

CHUNGKI JUNGLE CAMP

Jim and his mates were so tired that many of them just fell to the floor of the huts and went straight to sleep while others spoke about the horrors of the day they had just spent. Most of them spoke of how they were going to make themselves a good bed out of bamboo tomorrow, but they were to have no time for this as early next morning they were awoken while it was still dark and rounded up into work parties. They were given their half cup of rice and a cup of hot muddy water to drink, then marched off into the jungle to start work. As they marched dawn broke and as they came to a clearing that other prisoners had already cleared, they saw more Jap guards standing by some huts. On seeing the prisoners coming the Jap guards opened up the huts and brought out tools such as picks and shovels, and an assortment of native tools. Many of the chaps had no idea what they were for but knew they would soon find out.

The men's task was to build up a railway embankment; they started work straight away and were allowed two rest breaks a day (or 'Yasumi' in Japanese). During this rest time, which was about twenty minutes to half an hour if they were lucky, they were given another cup of rice and cup of hot water, on this they worked 'til nine o' clock at night. Then they faced their march back to camp where they would just fall asleep through sheer exhaustion, ready to face the same thing the very next day. Jim was put in a work party clearing rocks. He and about ten other chaps were with a Japanese engineer who would set charges in the rocks and blow them up then Jim and his mates would load the rocks and boulders into man made stretchers carried by two other prisoners who would carry them to where the other prisoners were building the railway embankment. The Jap engineer was a Judo fanatic and Jim and his mates were used as bait by him but they found this gave them a break from work, and the Jap did teach them how to fall, but they

34

still received many bruises. They did not mind this too much but they did fear being cut for the smallest cut could turn into a tropical ulcer and all of them had seen chaps lose legs through them and many men died through the operation and lack of aftercare. It turned out the Jap had been to Cambridge University to study engineering and sometimes to make the men feel home sick he would say how nice it would be to be walking down Regent Street in Cambridge or having a drink in one of the pubs in town, of which he seemed to know all the names. He told them how he had done the King Street run consuming a pint at each pub and how ill he had been the next .day, to which the lads thought to themselves 'pity it never killed him!'.

The Japanese officer in charge of Chungki camp had a great hatred of the British and would have worked the men to death if he could; he would demand more work to be done every day – he even had gas lights set up so that the men could work on well into the night. Jim and his mates were working eighteen hours a day now, and this was telling on the men who were not fit to start with. All of this on two cups of rice a day. Sickness was all around now and Jim knew that he and his mates could not last like this for much longer, suffering from attacks of malaria, dysentery and beri-beri, through malnutrition and no vitamins. They had dermatitis, ringworm and even outbreaks of cholera which took men very quickly , yet even this did not stop thc Japs from making the men work. They would pull men out of the hospital hut and if they could stand they were fit for work. Many who could not stand were kicked and beaten where they fell, and many of these men died from the beatings they received as they were already so weak from sickness. It did no good the British officers complaining or quoting the Geneva Convention – this just angered the Japs more, and more beatings were handed out and officers ordered to work or be shot.

On returning to camp one evening one of the Korean guards did not like the way Jim looked at him, and pushed Jim to the ground. Jim rolled himself up into a ball like a hedgehog, expecting a kicking and beating to follow, but instead he was pulled to his feet and made to stand upright with his hands above his head; the guards placed a heavy boulder in his hands and he was made to stand like this while being prodded by the guards. He was left like this until he collapsed from exhaustion. His mates were allowed to drag him away to their hut where they did what they could to help him. Jim from then on always kept his head down not wanting to make eye contact with the guards in case they picked on him again for no reason, but he soon found out the guards did not need any reason – they just snatched at anyone to dish out their cruelty for their amusement.

The long days of hard work carried on and now the rains had set in – it rained non stop for days on end, all day and all night, but still the men were expected to turn out the same amount of work as when conditions were dry. The conditions were very bad – the camp was flooded causing the latrines to flow through the huts, raw sewage was all over the place, men had nowhere dry to sleep and were up to their knees in water and sewage. After a few days like this the Japanese did move some of the men to a Thai village and took over a school that was built up on poles some five or six feet above the ground; the men were just pleased to have somewhere dry to lay after their hard days work. Once conditions improved and the camp dried out the men were all taken back to clean up the huts and dig fresh latrines and most important to put fresh dried leaves on their beds; all of this after a hard day's work of course. They were given post cards to send home to their families. The cards were already written out and Jim and his mates were asked to cross out three out of the four lines which were: I AM WELL; I AM WORKING FOR PAY; I AM IN HOSPITAL; I HAVE RECEIVED RED CROSS PARCEL. Jim left the line saying 'I AM WELL' which most of the men did, even though many of them died within days of sending these cards. Jim was getting about a penny a day in our money (about a dollar a fortnight) with which the chaps bought what extras they could from local traders to help their poor diet; also they were now catching snakes which after skinning and cooking tasted something like chicken. This all helped top up their twice-a-day rice ration.

After Christmas 1942, for which Jim and his mates got the day off to pass as they liked within the camp, Jim attended church in one of the atap huts to sing carols and pray for better days to come and for their families back home whom Jim imagined sitting at home tucking into their roast turkey and all the trimmings. How his mouth watered at the thought of it and how it would be washed down with a nice glass of beer. He thought of how he and his father used to go to their local pub, the Red Bull on Barton Road, Newnham for a couple of pints before dinner and wondered if his dad was well and would be going to the pub this Christmas without him. He sat and had a quite tear to himself as he thought of his loved ones back home and said a special prayer for all of them. January 1943 came and Jim and his mates were rounded up again and, carrying all their tools and things, were marched off further into the unknown to another camp further on up the line – the Thailand to Burma railway they were constructing followed the line of the Kwai river. Many of the men were too weak to march and the fitter ones helped them along with plenty of smacks around the head from the guards. Many men suffering from dysentery were left to catch up at their own pace. They arrived at camp Wun Lun and spent one night there. Early next morning they marched off again stopping at camp Wan Tai Kin for the night.

Chapter Eight

MOVING DOWN THE LINE

The men exchanged stories with men already in the camp and some met up with pals they had been parted from back in Singapore. They exchanged stories of sabotage, of how they would place wood instead of ballast in the railway embankment so as to weaken it, those in bridge building parties told of their tales of sabotage and they hoped they never had to use it. They reassured one another by saying 'the Japs won't let us ride on any train – they would rather force-march us while their troops use the railway,' but before long the railway was being used bringing more prisoners from Changi and parts of Singapore to work on the railway. Jim and his mates were soon having a train ride which took them to Tamarkan camp. Here Jim saw many of his friends die from cholera and he and the others had the job of burning their bodies in mass fires. Men would be all right at breakfast time, feel ill in the morning, and be dead by night fall from it. Jim lived in fear of catching it and washed all over in the disinfectant issued by the Japs to spray the huts with to help prevent its spread, for this was one thing the Japs were scared of. Jim was never to forget the sight of the mens' bodies sitting upright while in the fire and looking straight at him as the heat from the fire contracted their muscles. Many of these men were Jim's mates, and this at times was just to much for Jim to bear.

Jim was soon moved back to Chungki camp and back to the rock blasting party. One day his work party, consisting of about ten men with one Jap guard, were trying to move a large boulder from the top of a rock face. They had large wooden poles that were being used as wedges and levers to push the boulder over the rock face to below, which was about a thirty foot drop, where men were waiting to smash it up into ballast. Jim and his mates could not quite get the boulder to roll over the cliff face; the Jap guard could see this and rather than send for more prisoners from below he gave a hand to push it over the edge; the men and the guard gave one big effort and the boulder went, but just as the boulder went over, the Jap guard lost his footing and followed the boulder over the edge landing head first on the rocks below. All the prisoners stood in horror – those below looking up at Jim and his mates wondering if Jim and the others had pushed him over. He was dead. He lay there with his skull smashed wide open and within seconds Jap guards were all over the place handing out beatings. Jim and the other men from the top were beaten on the spot and all of them thought 'this is it – they are bound to think we pushed him over'. Jim and the others were taken back to camp and were left standing with their arms above their heads until they just collapsed and as each man did so they were dragged away on their own by the Jap guards and were questioned by Jap officers then given back to the guards for more ill treatment. This went on for some days during which three of the men died from the beatings, but on the evening of the fourth day a Jap officer told Jim and the other six men that were left that he believed their story of what had happened to the guard, and that they would be allowed to live. Jim and the others were taken to sick hut where the medics did what they could for them. They were allowed two days off work to recover from the ordeal. Jim had taken such a beating that he thought to himself that it might be better to just let go and die as he felt so low. Through the help of one Jap guard who Jim felt had truly tried to help him and the others move that boulder, four men were dead. As Jim lay in the sick hut with his thoughts of death, he slipped into a deep sleep. He awoke two days later to hear the medical doctor say "welcome back, Jim".

The doctor got Jim and the other six men off work duty as they were in a bad way, but that did not stop the Japs making them parade every morning to see if they were fit for work. Men who could hardly stand were expected to work. The Japs were so cruel, having no thought of the mens' suffering. It meant nothing to them if the men lived or died. All they thought about was getting the railway finished. Jim had taken such a bad kicking to his legs that they ulcerated and this was to be a problem to Jim in the days of his captivity. Jim started to feel stronger – after a few days he was even given sugar while in the sick hut and this was just heaven to him. To be able to have a cup of tea with sugar in was such a luxury and the food in the sick hut was so much better. They had meat with their rice, and some days they had fresh fruit. After a few days of this luxury Jim was passed fit and was soon marching back to the quarry for more rock blasting but after a few weeks of this his legs were so ulcerated he was back in the sick hut from where he was later sent to Tamarkan sick camp for more treatment to his leg ulcers which were now so bad that you could see the bone in his legs. Jim had used maggots to eat the bad rotting flesh from the ulcers and on arrival at the camp Jim was taken to the ulcer ward, which was just a plain bamboo hut with a long bamboo bench running its length and about a foot from the floor suspended by larger bamboo struts. The stench was so bad it made Jim sick. As he lay on the bamboo bench which was to be home to him for the next six weeks, another prisoner came to him and told him "I'm your medic and I have to wash and change your dressings twice a day" but as there were no new bandages the same ones had to be washed out each time and re-used. Jim was once again given better food and some vitamins to help build him up.

Jim was one of the lucky ones and responded to treatment, but many of the men who arrived with Jim lost their legs because of the ulcers – some even never recovered from the operations, conditions were so bad. Jim compared the conditions to the times he had read about in the American civil war and the pictures he had seen of soldiers biting on a bit of wood while a surgeon cut their leg off with a saw, while the patient lay on an old wooden table covered in blood. Nothing had changed, for this is just how Jim's fellow prisoners-of-war were being operated on, but as Jim knew, the medical men were doing the best they could with the resources available to them. As Jim got better he knew once again he had survived because of the bravery of fellow prisoners who would break out of camp and buy what medical supplies they could from the Thais just to help those in the ulcer ward. Jim, like many of the others, knew they would never be able to repay these brave men who had risked their own lives to save theirs.

Jim was soon passed fit for work and was sent off again further into the jungle to carry on working on the railway. He was moved up line to Wampo. He was still feeling very ill, as were many of the others, and his friends helped him as much as they could, but once again they were loaded into steel-sided trucks when the heat of the day was unbearable for them. Many of the men, including Jim, were suffering from malaria and dysentery and most of them had some kind of skin diseases and beri-beri, but still the Japs were sending them off to do more hard work. The train set off and Jim and his mates made themselves as comfortable as they could by sitting on their old rice sacks that also served as their bed blanket. The train travelled at only about 5 miles an hour for fear of derailment, which was very common. Also the men knew that their fellow prisoners of war who had built this part of the railway, like themselves, would try to sabotage parts of it by whatever means they could. Because of this the men feared derailment at any time; they had heard many stories of how many prisoners had lost their lives due to derailment as it was now common practice for the Japs to make prisoners be the first to travel over any newly completed part of the railway – this was the Jap's way to stop sabotage. Jim and his mates soon found they were not the first to travel on this section of the railway when they passed by a derailment where two trucks had left the rails and had fallen down the ten foot embankment. The train seemed to go even slower to Jim and his mates now, and they laughed together that the Jap train driver must be as scared as they were. As they passed along they passed near to many of the prison camps and saw work parties of prisoners and natives working on the embankments to the railway line.

The men had no chance to boil the drinking water on this trip and so were having to drink the water just as it came from the rivers so of course this did not help Jim or his mates with their dysentery and sickness and once again all they had to eat was their half a tea cup of rice twice a day. When they stopped for half an hour most of the men were just glad to stretch their legs but for many of them they were just too ill to stand, let alone walk about. Jim had to force his few mouthfuls of rice down as he felt so ill – all he wanted to do was sleep but his mates would help him along by walking each side of him with Jim's arms around their shoulders for support. They knew this would help keep Jim's muscles working and keep the blood flowing through his bad legs; they used to say "come on Jim, the trains stopped, time to stretch your legs mate". Jim would reply "just let me sit here lads, its not worth getting out just for half an hour". "Come on with you," his mates would reply, "some fresh air and to stretch your legs will give you an appetite for your dinner" at which Jim could not help but laugh, even though he felt so ill. "I don't need rice" he would say, "I just wish I could have some nice roast beef, roast potatoes and veg and a nice cold beer to wash it down with". His mates would say "that's what we would all like, Jim, but we ain't gonna get it old mate, so just eat that rice and think it's what you would like it to be!".

After a few days they arrived at Wampo. Wampo was a part of the railway that ran round the side of the mountain, built on very large timber supports and made up of tiers of wooden supports constructed onto the river bed below. In places it was some sixty foot above the river and it really was an engineering feat in itself. Jim and his mates were taken to another atap hut which had no flooring to it – just a mud floor which was crawling with bugs, insects etc. The men were so tired and so ill they just laid on their old rice sacks and slept. They were woken very early next morning, paraded outside and counted then split into work parties. Those who said they were too sick to work were just pushed into line by the Jap guards and told "no work no food." Most of them, fearing a beating, got into line with the help of a friend who was not feeling too bad. They then had a five mile march from their jungle camp to the railway they had to work on – the Wampo viaduct. The job they were given to do was the strengthening of the timber supports. Jim was much too weak for this work as it meant climbing down the wooden structure of the viaduct some forty feet above the ground below, and one slip through not being able to hold on meant certain death if one fell.

Chapter Nine

ON TO TAKUNUN

Jim and his mates spent a week on the viaduct work at Wampo, but most of them were so weak they just could not manage the work set them. Furthermore the Allied planes were now coming over on bombing raids, and though this was good to see it also brought much danger to the men, not just from the fear of the bombing from their own side but from the panic from the Jap guards. They allowed the prisoners to move just ten feet if an attack came but they themselves would run for the nearest cave. On one such occasion Jim was working some sixty feet above the ground right in the middle of the viaduct with about half a mile each side of him to go to get back to level ground. On hearing the planes the Jap guards just set off running for cover. Jim knew it was no good him and the other prisoners running anywhere so he just hung on tight to a railway sleeper by just wrapping his arms and legs round it but he saw one poor chap just knocked clean off the viaduct by one of the Jap guards who just shoulder-barged him clean out of the way as the Jap ran for cover, which meant jumping from one sleeper to the next. The poor chap who was pushed off of course died from the fall and was buried in the jungle. One of the chaps made a wooden cross from one of the railway timbers and carved out the man's name on it and added the date of his death. Jim read his bible reading and the men all joined in singing 'Abide With Me', then they all filed by the grave saying their last goodbyes to their friend and were then marched back to camp saying to one another that their friend was at least free from all the suffering . The men all found it hard to sleep that night with thoughts of their lost friend and wondering where they were off to now. It seemed just as they did get to sleep they were woken by the Jap guards and paraded outside and counted. They gathered what possessions they had and were then marched off once again, the stronger men helping the weaker ones.

After marching along for some miles they at last boarded the steel railway trucks again and were glad to be able to sit down. They were informed they were moving on to Takunun camp nearer to Burma. Jim was now very ill and his mates were very concerned for him; he would not eat and was feeling so ill he just wanted to give up. On arrival at Takunun, Jim was allowed to be taken to the sick hut where his friends laid him on fresh dried leaves on a bamboo platform and told the medic "do your best for him please." As they left him there they all thought he would be dead by the morning – Jim was suffering from spinal malaria, yellow jaundice, beri-beri, and still had dysentery. His weight had dropped from thirteen and a half stone on arriving at Singapore to five and a half stone now. He was just like a skeleton who could not walk but just managed to crawl on all fours. The medical orderly saved his life by slapping Jim's face to keep him from falling into a coma, and once again Jim was saved by someone's bravery. A Dutch prisoner was so pleased to hear that Jim's surname was spelt the same as his that he volunteered to do extra work to his after working all day on the railway. He would do extra work to earn extra food for Jim to help him get well again.

After many weeks Jim did start to get well, and yet still the Dutch man worked extra just to get extra things to help Jim; he would sit with Jim bathing his head to keep him cool. Once Jim was feeling better and could talk again, he told the Dutch man "I can never repay your kindness to me – you by your unselfishness have kept me alive. I shall never forget you," to which the Dutch man replied "to have a name as rare as mine makes you my brother, Jim. God bless and keep you safe always. I'm just pleased to have met you and to see you well is all I wanted, as I am being moved on soon and now I can go knowing that you have come through." The two men embraced one another and cried out their emotions and told one another that after the war they would meet in better circumstances and become even better friends.

When the Dutch man left, Jim lay thinking of how near he had come to death. He had once again looked it right in the face and through the grace of God had escaped its grasp once more. He thought what a miracle it was that a total stranger to him would do so much for him just because they shared the surname of Bentinck. As he lay there, his emotions running high, he thought of his days at Sunday school when he was a young boy back home in Newnham which now seemed a world away. The one story that came to his mind was of Jesus telling the story of the Good Samaritan for that is how Jim thought of the Dutch man. Now he lay thinking once again of his loved ones back home and said to himself 'I must recover and get back to them and one day we shall all be together again.' Jim slipped off to sleep that night a happy man dreaming of home.

He soon started to make progress and got back to six and a half stone in weight and was put back on light work. He also found that the Jap officer in charge of the camp was much the best he had come across to date – he did try to improve their living quarters and the food but the best rations did not seem to get to the camp and the Japanese officers and guards were living on the same as the prisoners. This helped the men's morale and rumours spread round the camp that the allies must be starting to win the war. A recci plane had been over most days and the men were sure something was going to happen. Jim was now passed fit to work and he resumed work again and was put with some of his old mates. Again their job was to replace broken sleepers on the railway line, and repair the embankments where there had been a derailment. Sometimes even replacing a section of rail Jim was amazed to see that the Jap guards worked along with them and this made the men feel much better. They soon got to know which Japs they could trust and those they had to watch out for, one of whom the men called Gold Rush – this was because he had a mouth full of gold teeth and the men would say to one another how they would love to smack him in the mouth and knock his teeth out and collect all the gold. Jim used to say "yes, it would make up for some of the gold rings and necklaces they took from me back in Singapore, that I had for my family back home." The men knew if they were picked for his work party that they would get no rest periods and at least one of them could expect a beating from him. Jim knew from how he felt that another beating would kill him and so he lived in fear of being put into his work party. Jim still did not make eye contact with the Japs for he still remembered the beating he had received for looking at one of the guards before. One evening as the men got back to camp and were preparing their meal of rice and monkey stew, (it was a nice clear evening in December 1944) all of a sudden the men heard the drone of aeroplane engines and soon saw bombers overhead – twenty or more in all. The men forgot about their food and said to each other "someone's in for it – they must be off to Singapore." While the men stood watching them go off into the distance, they saw several of the bombers break formation and swing round heading back towards them. They stood in amazement has they saw the bomb doors open and the sound of bombs start to fall. Jim and the others just ran with the Japs into the surrounding jungle and hid wherever they could as bombs fell all around them. It went on for what seemed for ever to the men, who now feared they were going to be killed by their own side. They could not believe that after all they had been through they could now be killed by their own allied bombers, and this was all they could think of as the bombers flew off .

Once the bombers had left, the Japs and the prisoners came slowly out of the jungle; the Japs were very frightened – for many of them it was the first time they had come under enemy fire, and it was clear to the men that the Japs did not like it. They called a quick roll call and after much counting found that men were missing. The rest of the night was spent helping the Japs find the missing prisoners. Several prisoners were found dead and some Japanese guards had been killed as well. The men formed burial parties and set to to bury their dead. They made wooden crosses and placed large stones on the graves in the hope of stopping animals from digging up their dead comrades. Not much sleep was taken that night – most of the men were either too shocked or too excited to sleep. Many thought that the end of their suffering would soon be over now that the allies were bombing and fighting back, but many of them feared being killed by their own men bombing them or by the Jap guards killing them to prevent anyone knowing how the Japanese had treated them.

While they lay talking, the dawn came up and they were mustered up and counted once more, then they were put into work parties and marched off into the jungle to clear away trees that had come down in the bombing raid and had fallen across the railway lines; some parts of the railway had taken direct hits . Jim's work party were marched some twenty miles in all along the railway line repairing the embankment and removing fallen trees from the line. As they were some miles from camp they spent a few nights sleeping at the edge of the jungle as the Japs wanted to get repairs done as quickly as possible so as to get their troops moving again up to Burma to where the action was.

Being away from camp meant food was bad. All the Japs had brought along was rice – no stew to go with it. As the Jap guards were working with the prisoners and how they were on the same rations, they allowed some of the men to hunt animals from the jungle to top up their food ration of rice. Snakes and monkeys were caught and cooked up and the men were only too pleased to have some meat with their rice. Jim found the snake tasted much like chicken but the monkeys could be quite tough and Jim always liked to watch the monkeys swinging through the trees – he thought of them as more human than the Japs and so thought it was not right to be eating them. The day was divided into eighteen hours of work and six hours sleep. On the second evening away from camp the men heard the allies' bombers again. Work stopped and everyone looked up to see some thirty odd bombers going over. They soon heard the sound of the bombs exploding and said to one another "wonder who's getting that lot." It was not long before the bombers came back, their mission over for that night.

Next morning, Jim and his mates were marched back to camp after being away about five days. They saw their mates were digging a large ditch around the camp's perimeter and banking all the earth up to form a large embankment right round the camp. Jim and his work party were sent into the jungle to bring back vegetation to place on the embankment so as to form camouflaging. This work went on for about a week. Now more and more bombing raids were coming over most days to bomb the bigger stations and bridges further down the line. Prisoners were being moved from camp to camp to help with repairs to the railway lines and news reached Jim and his mates that many of the main bridges had been bombed but that many prisoners had been killed because of this. On hearing this the men tried to do whatever they could to mark parts of the camp to let the bomber pilots know it was a prison camp. Jim and his work party were soon on the move again – they were being sent further up line to carry out more repairs.

They carried their work implements with them as they marched along the railway line, stopping for about a days work at a time to repair embankments and twisted railway lines before marching off to the next bombing damage. The men were all very weak and they laughed to one another how they might make one good healthy bloke out of two of them put together. They were still supplementing their diet with whatever they could. They came across a party of natives working on part of the railway and were told they must not talk to any natives – any one caught talking to them would be killed. This only made Jim and his mates think that the Japanese must be losing the war now and that the natives must know this. Why else couldn't they talk to one another? They worked along with the natives and Jim was pleased to see some on elephants which were used to pull the large trees along to make sleepers etc. Jim found the Japs were very cruel to the natives and saw many beatings handed out to them.

The Jap guards with Jim and his mates had now stopped working with them but at least they were not handing out beatings to them. One day while working up on the railway embankment lifting in new sleepers Jim and another prisoner slipped and fell down the eight foot embankment to the ground below just as two elephants were coming by. Jim fell flat on his back and lay there dazed, which once again turned out to be lucky for him for the elephants just picked their feet up and stepped over him. Jim could not believe his luck. As he and the other prisoner picked themselves up they looked at one another wondering why they had not been crushed to death. They waved a sign of thank you to the two native boys who were riding on the elephants' backs, and then clambered back up the embankment to resume their work. Jim's mates said to him "you're a lucky old so and so – you must have nine lives." Jim replied "if not, I must have a guardian angel looking after me." As they worked on into the evening they saw more bombers come over them. This was getting regular now and there were not many nights when they did not catch sight of the bombers coming over to bomb the bigger stations and bridges down the line. They knew that many of their fellow captors would be killed in the raids and this was also a major worry to them all, for to have come through so much hardship and suffering just to die from being bombed by your own side was just about the worst that could happen.

One evening a train came by packed with natives – Thais, Malays and some Chinese. They had to stop as the line Jim and his mates were working on was what they needed to travel over. The natives were allowed to leave their carriages and stretch their legs while they waited for the work to be completed. Some of Jim's work party thought this would be their chance to find out if any of them had news of how the war was going on for they had all heard rumours that the allies had taken Singapore, but they could not be sure – perhaps the natives could let them know. They warned one another of the danger if any one was found talking to the natives, but one Englishman and one Dutchman said they would take that risk. They saw a young native girl sitting under a tree at the edge of the jungle about twenty yards away from them. The girl was talking to two older men, and the other natives were walking about, so the Englishman and Dutchman thought if they could mix in with the natives and get to the jungle they could crawl on all fours up behind the native girl using the jungle background as camouflage. The two men let the Jap guard know they needed to go to the latrines because of dysentery but now that they were not at any camp, the men just used to squat down in the jungle. The Jap guard just pointed to the jungle and grunted in broken English "you no be long." The two men went off. Once in the jungle they fell to the ground. The Dutchman said "I will keep watch, you crawl along behind the girl and try and find out what news they have." The Englishman crawled away and came up behind the girl who could not have been more than twenty years old. The two native men had moved away from her now and she lay alone. The Englishman started to talk to her, but Jim and the others never knew what he found out, for what Jim was about to witness in the next few hours was to be one of the worst nightmares he would ever have. One of the Jap guards noticed the girl laying on her own and started to walk towards her, probably thinking to himself some indecent thoughts of things he could do with her. On seeing the Jap guard approach, the Dutchman called out to the Englishman and the Dutchman walked out of the jungle as if he had just been answering a call of nature, but as he called out the young native girl jumped up, startled. This only made the Jap guard rush towards her. When he saw the Englishman laying face down he turned and knocked the girl to the ground, and started kicking out at the Englishman. By this time other Jap guards were on the scene and the girl and the English prisoner were taken away. The Dutchman was able to return back to the work party, still fearing for his life in case the Japs found out he was in on the event. A few hours passed with everyone wondering what was happening to the English and native prisoners who were taken by the Japs into one of the rail trucks for questioning. When they reappeared looking badly beaten, the Japs summoned all the other prisoners to form a line along the side of the embankment. A Jap officer informed them all how they had been warned not to talk to one another and that now these two will be an example of what happens if you disobey Japanese orders. The Englishman was bent over, hands tied behind his back, and the Jap officer took out his large samurai sword and with one swing down took the mans head clean off. Jim shook with rage and fear as all his thoughts went back to all the terrible sights he had seen while driving the executioner but what he was to witness now was far worse – the girl was stripped naked and a stake was driven in the ground. Her legs were spread apart and staked to the ground so that she could not move them, then quick growing bamboo was placed beneath her private parts and placed inside her. She was then left for hours screaming in pain as the bamboo grew inside her while all the other prisoners were made to stand and watch. The sound of this poor girl's screams were to stay with Jim for the rest of his days. After hours of the poor girl's suffering the Jap officer chopped her head off, but was left tied to the post as a warning. Jim and the rest of the men were so shocked that no one spoke for hours – no one could eat or sleep, they were all so much in shock.

Over the next couple of days many fellow prisoners – truckloads of them – came by heading back down the line and Jim and his mates once more thought it must be nearly over. Why else would they be moving our boys back? Also, train loads of Jap Fighting Soldiers were coming the other way heading up to wards Burma. Jim and his work party were moved back to Takunun camp and were pleased to see their old friends again and exchange stories. Many of them had been moved down the line and the men wondered how long they would have to wait for their turn and would it bring the freedom they dreamed of. As they dreamed of their families back home they prayed that the day of freedom would not be far off now. Jim found that many men who did not believe in God were starting to pray and when Jim mentioned this to some of them they said "there must be someone, Jim. Perhaps that guardian angel of yours will look after us all."

Chapter Ten

CAMP TO CAMP

It was now the end of May 1945 and for the next three months Jim and his work party were moved from camp to camp repairing bomb damage to the railway line. The Japs in charge of Jim's work party were once again working alongside their prisoners, and this did help because while the Japs were working with them they did not hand out beatings – just the odd swipe with their pickle sticks to let Jim and his chums know who was in charge. Jim and his work party were moved up and down the line, passing through many of the camps, and taking news from camp to camp. They found that many of their fellow Cambridgeshires had died from malnutrition, beri-beri, tropical ulcers, cholera, dysentery, malaria, black river fever, rat plague, or by the beatings and unbearable cruelty handed out by the guards. Jim spent many nights in the jungle marching from one repair job to the next. The allied bombers were keeping them very busy now, by inflicting damage to the railway day and night. Many British prisoners were killed in these air raids.

Jim and his work party were moved back to Wampo Viaduct to help with bridge repairs. On arrival, Jim was amazed to see just how much damage had been done, and he wondered how he and his mates could even begin to carry out repairs. Most of the work party were to ill to work and Jim had gone from 13 stone 10 pounds down to 5 stone 8lbs., as had most of the men now with him. They knew that the work they were now expected to carry out at Wampo was just to heavy for them; to make matters worse it was monsoon time and the rains were flooding everywhere. They knew how slippery the rail sleepers would be and with, at times, a 60ft drop below them they knew even for fit men it would be dangerous. They worked day and night now, being allowed very little rest. The food was now worse than at any time, and Jim soon became to weak to stand. He was taken to Wampo hospital camp, suffering from malnutrition, dysentery, malaria and beri-beri, yet still every morning he would be forced to his feet by the Jap guards and lined up outside with the rest of the patients. If they could not stand on their own the Jap sergeant would beat them with his hard bamboo pickle stick, and if those who could stand did not salute him they too received a beating. Many sick men died at the hands of this Jap.

Some time in July most of Jim's party were moved down line to Tamuang camp but Jim was so ill he could not remember if he was moved or not. Then in August he was told the war was over and that they would soon have the proper medication to get him well. The other men made large union jacks and placed them over the camps so that they could be seen from the air and it was not long before leaflets were dropped by air to let all Allied prisoners-of-war know that the Japanese had surrendered and that the war was over. Men reacted in many ways – some could not control their emotions and just cried and cried, for others it came as such a shock that they suffered heart attacks and died on the spot, and others felt like taking revenge on Japs, but their officers informed them that war crimes would be dealt with through the proper channels, and that order and discipline must be maintained. Jim was still too ill to take it all in – when friends visited him and read the leaflet to him he was pleased for them all but he himself felt so ill he just could not take it in. Over the next few days, air drops of food and medication were dropped to the camps, and at last the medics had the medication and good food to get Jim and the others better.

Chapter Eleven

FREE AT LAST

Over the next few weeks Jim received very light food and plenty of good vitamins and medication to treat his illnesses, and at last he started to feel a bit better and the will to live came back to him, but he was still very ill and when his mates started leaving to prepare for home Jim felt so sad not to be with them, for all he wanted now was to get home to see his loved ones again – that would be the tonic he needed to get him well again. Some air mail had got through and one letter was for Jim. One of the medics read it to him as his eyes were not up to reading because of his condition. It was from his father saying how it would not be long 'til they would be together again. These were the first words written by any of his family that Jim had heard in almost four years and Jim could not control his emotions and just cried like a baby. The medic said "let it all out, Jim." As he comforted him the two men sat and spoke of their homes to one another and of their dreams for the future.

The medical officers were now preparing the men to be moved. They were sorted into three categories – A, B and C. The first group were men who could be moved straight away, the second group were men who could be moved but with medical care, and group C were those men who must get to a hospital as soon as possible. This final group was the one Jim was put in. Jim could not remember too much of the journey as he was sedated, but some of the journey was made by rail and by boat until they arrived at the nearest air field, where they were loaded onto Dakota transport planes and flown to Rangoon to be taken to hospital. Jim did remember that the pilot of the Dakota he was on was the young American actor Mickey Rooney who took the time to come back and wish them all the best once they had landed. Once Jim got to hospital he soon got on – he put weight on and started to feel much better. He was visited by Lord Mountbatten whom he found very helpful; he answered Jim's questions and explained how things were going to get them home again. Jim was moved to a transit camp in mid September and within a few days was on board ship and on his way. The voyage was good with fine weather, fine comrades to travel with, much to talk about, but above all, lots of good food and medication. Jim could not believe just how well he was getting on – he was putting on weight and was feeling fitter every day; the sea air suited him, he was never sea sick and this also helped him get on better then some. He was pleased that by the time his loved ones would see him that he would have put on even more weight. He thought back to how just a few weeks before, he had been just a skeleton, who could not even walk. He knew if the war had not ended when it did he would not be here, for if those medical supplies had not been dropped into his camp he would have not got better. He sat thinking over the past four years and of the times he had escaped death. He sat and gave a short prayer to thank God for that guardian angel that had looked over him through those dark days, and he prayed for all his loved ones back home and for a better future for them all.

It was mid-October 1945 when Jim reached England once again. It was cold and foggy, but what a sight for Jim to see England at last. He stood with tears running down his face as he looked at dear old England. As they docked they could hear the people cheering them home and Jim and the others knew just how lucky they were. They had a silent moment together thinking of their friends and comrades who had not made it, those who had been killed in those first few weeks in action in Singapore, and those who had died on that death railway and whose bodies were buried in a jungle in a foreign land – many more who had died of tropical illnesses would never see home again.

Tele: WARWICK 650 Extn. 34.   Ref: V/112/XJ/1131.

To ..Pte....Bentinck...B.

....
....

     I wish to take this opportunity of expressing the pleasure of the Officers and Staff of this Record Office at your safe arrival from a Prison Camp, and hope that now you are at home again you will soon be restored to health.

     In case you are feeling 'lost' and wondering to whom you belong, I have to inform you that while you are in hospital, or if you are on leave, the Officer i/c Records is to be regarded as your Commanding Officer. As such he takes a personal interest in the welfare of all his men and it will help him to do so if you keep him advised of any important changes of address, or changes of next-of-kin, or anything that may be necessary. In any letter you send to this Office you should always state that you are a Repatriated Prisoner of War, and quote the above reference number.

     The following information is being forwarded to you so that you need have no anxiety concerning any matter which may occur during your repatriation leave.

     Any questions concerning Pay, Credits, and Allowances should be addressed to the Regimental Paymaster at Ilfracombe, not to this department.

     If you have received no instructions by the end of your leave, you should remain at home and await such instructions. You are assured that these will be sent to you in due course.

     A medical board will be arranged for you very shortly. It is pointed out that it is for your own benefit that your state of health may be determined, and you should make every effort to attend.

     If you require any further advice or assistance, you should write to or call at the following address:-

.....152...R.A.C..............
...Cpperton..PK...............
.........Herts................

which is the unit to which you are attached whilst on leave. (You do NOT have to report there upon the termination of your leave).

     A pamphlet explaining all about Civil Resettlement is enclosed.

     It is notified for your information that paid and unpaid acting ranks and paid and unpaid lance appointments have to be relinquished on 62nd day after disembarkation.

Colonel,
O.i/c Infantry Record Office.

WARWICK.
9-11-1945

Chapter Twelve

HOME AT LAST

As they landed to the cheers of the crowds they fastened up their Army great coats to keep the cold out. After years of tropical heat they were now in England's cold, damp October. When Jim realized what the date was he remembered it was his mother's birthday. He was informed that all nearest family would be informed they were home and Jim thought that will be a great present for his Mum. He and the others were taken to transit camps where they stayed for two or three days for further medicals to be done on them, before they were allowed leave for home. While at the camp, mail that had not got through to them before was given to them. Jim received letters from his parents, his fiancé and her mother, and also one from the two girls and their father whom he had met all those years ago as a child when he threw the stone at their window; also one from his young cousin. As he sat reading the letters he knew it would not be long now before he could see them all face to face and embrace them once more. That day soon came – he was issued his train pass, given some money and sent on his way.

When he arrived at Cambridge station it was a dream come true. It seemed so much better now; before, when he had come to Cambridge station, it was to come home on a 48 hour pass or to be going back to his unit again, but now he was home and how good that station looked to him. Now he got straight to a taxi and said "take me to number 1 South Green Road, Newnham, as fast as you can, please." He chatted to the taxi driver who told him of the damage Cambridge had received. They soon reached Jim's home where all his loved ones had gathered to greet him. I leave you to imagine the scene and the emotions that were exchanged in that house that day.

Jim went on to be demobbed and settled back into post-war life in England, although he was still not a fit man. He soon found work driving again and never received any war pension due to his injuries or the tropical diseases he suffered, about which Jim always felt bad. He suffered the rest of his life with tropical worms in his blood, and from malaria-type fevers and chills. His left leg that suffered so badly from tropical ulcers was just like bone with most of the calf muscle missing, but he never complained – like so many of those brave men, they just got on with life for they had already been to hell and back.

Jim was pleased to be invited on Thursday 20th December 1945 to a Civic Reception at the Guildhall, Cambridge by the Mayor. He was allowed to take three friends as guests. He took his wife-to-be, Dulcie, and two friends, and with what strength he had left they danced away the evening enjoying life once again as young people should. He and his fellow Cambridgeshires were given the Freedom of Cambridge. Jim felt honoured to receive this for many people did not know of the suffering they had been through as they received much more information of the war in Europe than they did from the Far East, which made Jim and his mates feel like the forgotten Army at times, but now at least the Cambridge people were honouring them. Jim was the only chap to return to Newnham – all his mates from school had died in the war in Europe or somewhere near Jim in the Far East. He spent time visiting the families of those who had been killed with him to reassure them of how their sons or loved ones had been buried. He explained to them how if he was on burial duties he always prayed over them and sang the Cambridgeshires' hymn, 'Abide With Me' and made a cross for their graves.

Jim was married to Dulcie in 1946 at Impington Church, a day he thought he would never see. Many of his Army friends attended and a great day was had by all. Jim had mentioned to the vicar just how lucky he felt to be able to be getting married that day, as it was something that he had dreamed of during those dark days in the Far East, and the vicar mentioned this during the service, and a minute's silence was held for everyone to remember those brave men who had given their lives for their King and Country. Jim never, ever forgot how lucky he had been to be spared. He spent the rest of his life helping others – he worked as a lorry driver for the National Benzol petrol company, and for Milk Vessels Recovery Ltd. for his first love was always driving. But the last fifteen years of his working life he spent as a security guard for the Cambridge Newspapers Group. He also spent twenty five years as a Special Constable, working evenings and weekends for the Cambridge Police Force.

After getting married, Jim and Dulcie lived with her parents in Impington, who were both invalids. They also had Dulcie's grandmother living with them and they soon found the house was not big enough for them so they moved to the adjoining village of Histon and bought a large old farm house with two acres of land where they worked the land, kept pigs, chickens etc and paid their mortgage off with the money they made from the proceeds. With both of them in full time work, they never had much spare time. However, they must have found some time to enjoy one another's company for in June 1949 Dulcie gave birth to a son. This was another dream come true for Jim. He remembered back to those dark days and of how the Jap sniper had nearly shot off his wedding tackle and yet here he was holding his own new-born son. His son was christened Michael James and, yes, I am that son. I was to be the only child Jim and Dulcie had and I, like my dad, was brought up living with my grandparents. So I, like Jim, had lots of love in those lovely childhood days of the fifties.

As a young child I went with my dad to the Royal Albert Hall in London once a year to the Far Eastern Prisoners of War Remembrance Service. I shall never forget how men cheered men without legs, arms missing etc. When the Master of Ceremonies introduced army doctors to them, saying "I'm sure many of you will remember this doctor from such-and-such a camp who helped many of you keep alive when you thought your time had come" the men jumped up and down waving their walking sticks and crutches in the air, cheering these doctors like mad – a thing I shall never forget.

Jim was a member of his local Cambridge F.E.P.O.W. branch and he and mum spent many happy hours there with his old comrades enjoying a drink and a chat with them, but my dad would never speak about his time in the war to me until I was thirty years old; even then he would break down crying and we would sit and cry together but we wrote down notes of the things he had been through. I can honestly say that until I married and left home I can remember my dad having nightmares at least once a week and waking us all up through shouting out. He never received any medical help until he was sixty-five years old, when Mr. Don Few, a friend of dad's from the Cambridge Yasumi Club got him into Ely RAF hospital where doctors finally killed off the tropical worms in his blood. These were like large red round circles under the skin which would irritate like mad, but by pumping blood and drugs through him they finally killed them off .

Chapter Thirteen

HOME LIFE

Jim soon began to feel much better now that these worms had been killed off at last. He had now retired from work and was about to make one of his wife's dreams come true – she had always dreamed of visiting Singapore and Thailand to see where her Jim had been. As they had not made any plans through their working life for a pension and knew that they could not do much on their State pension, they sold their house and land and retired to Norfolk. With the money they made, the first thing Jim did was to take Dulcie to the Far East to show her the places he had been. They looked over many of the war cemeteries, finding many of the names of the lads Jim had been with, they travelled on the old railway line that Jim had helped to build, they visited the site where Jim had done so much rock blasting and the old cave was still there that Jim and his mates had taken shelter in during the Allied air raids towards the end of the war. Dulcie could see that this had moved Jim and so she left him for half an hour to be on his own with his memories to relive once again those terrible days of hardship and suffering. When he returned to Dulcie he was quiet and withdrawn; they held one another and cried tears of joy and gave thanks to God that they had enjoyed a life together, for all around them were reminders of those poor souls who had not made it.

After the first two weeks of visiting all the now historic sites, they settled back to enjoy their last week of this dream-come-true holiday just relaxing on the beaches and enjoying the food and the night life together. Many of the meals had rice in them and Jim would never eat rice – not after having nothing but rice for nearly four years, he had eaten his share of the stuff, he would say. Dulcie explained this to the hotel chef, and the chef went out of his way to prepare the same meals for Jim but without the rice; also when the hotel management found out that he and the party he was with had been Japanese prisoners-of-war they contacted Thailand Airways and paid the extra fares for Jim and his party to travel home first class – a flight Jim and Dulcie never forgot. His words to me on picking him up at Heathrow airport from the VIP lounge were "we could not have been looked after better, even if we had been Royalty." He explained to me how kind the Thailand people had been to them, and showed me the silk shirt they had hand made for him. I was just so pleased for them both. At least now they would have some happy memories to remember of the Far East.

My dad and I spoke much more now about his experiences of those dark days and he impressed on me the need to help one another, to remember the less fortunate and to remember one of his favourite sayings – 'there but for the grace of God go I.'

Over the next year my Dad was in and out of Ely RAF Hospital with health problems, and I cannot thank them enough for all they did for him and the many men like him. I only wish he had been to hospital years before, but when my mum did get him to go to his doctor (who, in his defence, was only a youngster) he told my dad that his worms were probably flea bites. My dad knew different, but not wanting to make a fuss he just put up with them, until his friend Don Few told him what they were and got him to go into Ely hospital. When he finished his treatment there we found that the doctors sorted dad out a small war pension but I think it was too late in coming – but as dad always pointed out to me, he was one of the lucky ones – he had come home. He always loved to attend the Cambridgeshires' Remembrance Service and march-past held at Ely Cathedral where the Cambridgeshires' colours standards are kept. He spent hours cleaning up his medals on these occasions and his clothes would have to be just so, with mum having to iron his trousers just before they would leave to go.

Jim had two grandchildren, Joanna and Scott, whom he worshipped. He was never happier than to be with them and when he was sixty seven years old I sat talking to him at my wife's fortieth birthday party. He sat watching them all dancing and enjoying themselves, and he said to me "if I was taken tomorrow, I could have no regrets, for you see, Mike, I've had all the things any man could wish for – I had a great childhood, I spent my young manhood years with some of the bravest men that ever lived, I've had the best wife a man could wish for, I've had you, son, and your lovely wife as the daughter I never had, and my two smashing grandchildren – just what more could I want? I've so much to be thankful for."

Jim was taken from us on the 6th of October 1990 after he suffered a massive heart attack. He was just 69 years old, but as he said, he had no regrets for he had had all the things any man could wish for. To us, his family that are left, we miss him so much but we were pleased that his passing was quick as he had suffered enough during those dark days at the hands of the Japanese.

These brave men must never be forgotten. Their lives have marked the paths of history and have kept us all free to enjoy the life we all sometimes take for granted. I pray for those that are left that they may be free from pain and that the Japanese Government will compensate them for their years of suffering before it's too late.

It is to all these brave men and those who shall grow not old as we that are left grow old, age shall not weary them, nor the years condemn them, at the going down of the sun, and in the morning, we will remember them.

For to them we owe so much. So this book is to their memory, and to my dad, my Hero.